P9-DDR-616

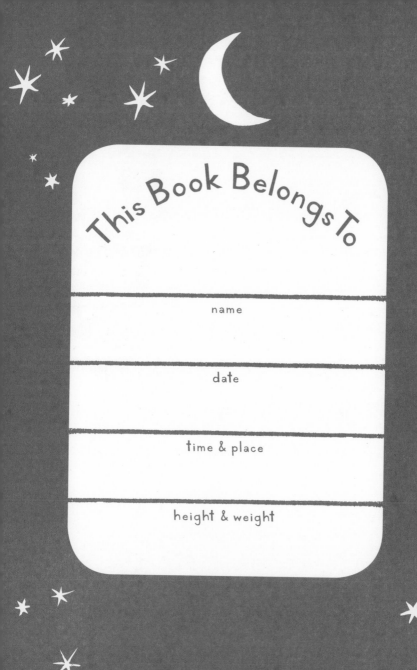

This Book Belongs To

name

date

time & place

height & weight

YOUR FAMILY TREE

THE STORY OF YOUR BIRTH

the first time I touched you and saw your fac

special memories of your birth

your first day, first visitors, first yawn

HOW WE
WELCOMED
YOU INTO
THIS WORLD

1 month

2 months

3 months

4 months

5 months

Make your own applesauce! Peel and cut apples, add a tiny bit of water and cook over low, mush, cool, eat with baby

7 months

8 months

9 months

10 months

11 months

12 months

HOW WE CELEBRATED

THIS SPECIAL DAY

SECOND YEAR

13 months

14 months

15 months

16 months

17 months

18 months

19 months

20 months

21 months

22 months

23 months

24 months

happy birthday!

BEYOND

all the new things you learn everyday,

new words, new skills, new friends

what you are curious about, what you like to eat,

how you spend your days, your many adventures

FIRST ADVENTURES
IN THIS WORLD

first boat ride, first city, first swim,

first bike ride, first blueberry

first friend, first steps, first ocean,

first walk around the block, first picnic

first party,
first tooth,
first bird,
first laugh,
first tree

first puddle, first rock, first leaf pile,

first squirrel, first pie, first rainbow

THE SONGS WE SING

songs for sleep,
songs for play,
songs we sing throughout the day,
songs you sing.

SONGS

THE GAMES WE PLAY

where's my baby?

spinning around, this little piggy, dance party

Silly things that make you laugh

THE BOOKS WE READ

first favorites, books we read over and over and o

ain, our special reading place, books you read on your own

THE WORK WE DO

salad making

the work we do together,
how we collaborate,
wiping your high chair,
washing clothes

HOW YOU HELP

sweeping the floor,
cleaning out the cupboards

THE TOOLS YOU USE

HOW YOU COMMUNICATE
& TELL YOUR STORIES

SIGNS YOU USE

the gestures you use, what you point at,

waving bye-bye, blowing kisses, all done!

FIRST WORDS

the sounds you make, words you know,

words you say, your voice, your first story

FIRST DRAWINGS

the marks you make

moon, cat, dog, baby, teapot, apple, flower, clock, boat, chicken

house,
tree,
spoon,
shoe,
eye,
ball,
bear,
fish,
chair,
bellybutton

ABC, yellow, red, blue, sun, umbrella, banana,

butterfly, fish, smiling faces

OUR DREAMS, WISHES
& HOPES FOR YOU

what we hope for your future,

adventures we want to go on with you

letter from parent

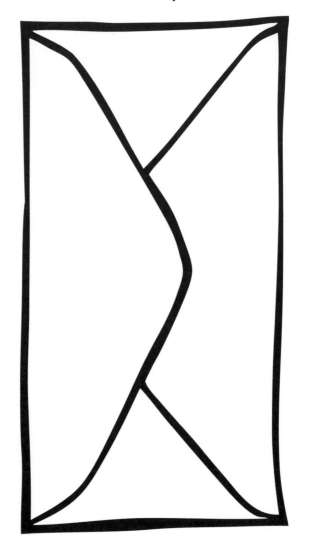

letter from parent

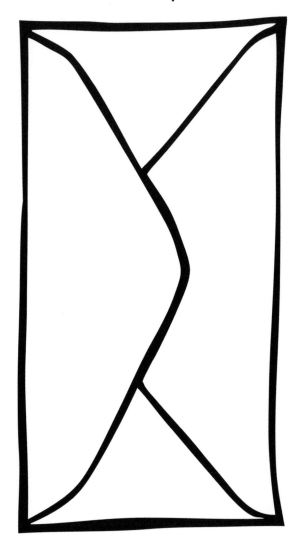

photos

hand tracing

About The Author

Nikki McClure of Olympia, WA, makes painstakingly intricate and beautiful paper cuts. Equipped with an X-Acto knife, she cuts out her images from a single sheet of paper and creates a bold language that translates the complex poetry of motherhood, nature, and activism into a simple and endearing picture. Her art can also be found in her annual calendar, notecard sets, and children's books.

Copyright ©2006 by Nikki McClure
All rights reserved. No portion of this book may be reproduced or utilized in any form, or by any electronic, mechanical, or other means without the prior written permission of the publisher.

Printed in China
Published by Sasquatch Books
17 16 15   13 12 11

Book design: Kate Basart/Union Pageworks

Library of Congress Cataloging-in-Publication Data is available.

ISBN 1-57061-508-X

ISBN 13:978-157061-508-5

Sasquatch Books | 1904 Third Avenue, Suite 710 | Seattle, WA 98101
206.467.4300 | www.sasquatchbooks.com | custserv@sasquatchbooks.com